"If I were a professional historian
I would try to show how little truth
I could tell in twelve volumes.
But being only an amateur,
I endeavor to put
the greatest number of facts
into the smallest
possible space.
I don't know all about history.
But to my best belief and knowledge
the things I tell are true
and I'm willing
to take an affidavit
to that effect.
This is a darned sight more
than most historians
will risk."

OSCAR AMERINGER

OSCAR AMERINGER

LIFE & DEEDS *of* UNCLE SAM

Introduction by Paul Buhle

Chicago
Charles H. Kerr Publishing Company
1985

On the cover:
"Uncle Sam Under Hypnosis"
(collage, 1983)
by Debra Taub

The text in this new edition of
The Life & Deeds of Uncle Sam
follows that of the original (1909) edition
except that a few outmoded ethnic epithets
have been changed in accordance with
Ameringer's own alterations
in later editions.

ISBN 0-88286-064-X
cloth 0-88286-065-8

Charles H. Kerr Publishing Company

P.O. Box 914
Chicago, Illinois 60690

594

Introduction

OSCAR AMERINGER, "the Mark Twain of American Socialism," once beloved by millions of readers in the midwest and southern coal towns, the southwestern prairies and throughout the American labor movement, has at last returned from an undeserved obscurity. We don't have Oscar himself—delightful columnist, hilarious speaker and dedicated radical—around anymore. But his autobiography, *If You Don't Weaken*, reprinted in 1983 by the University of Oklahoma Press, brings his personality back to light. *Life and Deeds of Uncle Sam* shows quite precisely how Ameringer managed to impart a sophisticated world-view to ill-educated readers through the use of "horse-sense" humor. No history book until Charles and Mary Beard's *Rise of American Civilization* reached so many readers. None yet has managed its economy of phrase or its iconoclastic shrewdness. Flaws notwithstanding, *Life and Deeds* remains the profound American example of making history come alive.

The booklet's subtle brilliance must be traced to the personality of Ameringer, the artist turned radical politician. He grew up in Swabia during the 1870s-80s, son of a cabinetmaker and freethinking mother. Instinctively, he turned against the reigning monarchy, and sought out the company of the hated village Jews, sharing with them pleasures of the forbidden, crypto-political "pulp" literature. His teachers judged him to have a future only at the end of a rope—or in America. A spiritual refugee in the New World, Ameringer spent his *Wanderjahre* as itinerant musician, portrait-painter, hobo playing his flute to the birds and riding the rails to some romantic destination. He grew to love the ordinary people and especially their enjoyment of a good joke, which he quickly learned to supply as the price for a meal, a sudden friendship, or a girl's kiss.

Ameringer perfected his English through study of a contemporary classic: *Mark Twain's Library of Humor*, actually a collaboration with William Dean Howells and Twain's Hartford friend George C. Clark. Here, some of the best-selling and finest American writing to date took on a collective dignity as the chief national contribution to world literature. Ameringer grasped the meaning for himself. Within months, he had successfully submitted to *Puck* "The Duke and His Dog," a satirical take-off on the wedding of a Cincinnati heiress and a British duke. European aristocracy offered an easy target, of course. But Ameringer aimed primarily at the American "shoddy aristocracy," a Gilded Age *nouveau riche* whose attempted imitation of European manners made them doubly ridiculous. This subject would provide a vast resource for ironic exploitation. Thirty years later, Ameringer was still mining the same vein for his own *Oklahoma Leader.*

> *This paper hasn't got a society editor yet so the boss asked me if I'd write something along that line. Here goes.*
>
> *Mat Climber, who has been in the supply business ever since he was old enough to carry a hod, is enjoying a well-deserved rest. Going home from somebody's place of business two weeks ago, he was run over by an automobile and has been laying around ever since.*
>
> *The ladies of the "Shakespeare Goodnight Club" held a literary at the country house of Mrs. Clarinda Potter Putundog. Miss Irene Highbrow, formerly of Bryn Mawr, delivered a masterly oratorical elocution on the Bard of Avon. She wore a Paris gown from the hips down. The body*

of the dazzling creation was composed of fleur de Lilly satin interspersed by chimpanzee lace and green poppies. The upper section of Miss Highbrow was dressed entirely in decollette with the exception of a wart in the right hand corner of her left shoulder blade.

These affairs will do much to further taste in belles lettres in our community and thus advance our literary standing. The next meeting of the club will be held at the Villa of Mrs. Amanda Derrick Crudeoil. Miss Crudeoil assured the members that in order to make her function a howling success she would spare neither time nor money to have Mr. Shakespeare appear in person.

Ameringer had learned well from the masters, and thereby joined the distinguished company of those select American humorists who turned their talent to radical ends. During the Revolutionary War, a handful of patriots had aimed literary barbs at the British. By Thomas Jefferson's account, newspaperman and poet Philip Freneau saved the emerging republic in the 1790s through exposing the monarchical intentions of Alexander Hamilton's crowd to withering ridicule. David Locke ("Petroleum Nasby"), Abraham Lincoln's favorite political writer, played an important role in the Civil War with his satires of pusillanimous Copperheads. Marietta Holley ("Samantha Allen") personally established a genre of proto-feminist humor in twenty-three popular volumes of attack upon male privilege. And Mark Twain himself, his pen dripping with acid, took on the post-Civil War society's corruption with an unforgettable vigor. At the end of his life, interviewed by the Kerr Company's own *International Socialist Review*, Twain confessed himself a closet socialist.

Ameringer belongs also to another school of radical

jokers, linked together by theme and style if often dimly aware of each other. The political repression and economic suffering of Europe brought many other rebels along with Ameringer to American shores. When immigrant workers mobilized their ranks to hold public meetings, publish newspapers or send out speakers to the neighborhoods and provinces, they selected the jack-of-all-trades intellectual spokesman. Agitator, educator, poet or novelist, he generally had a reputation for cracking a good joke. Some outstanding leaders made their name as political comics long before they convinced ordinary immigrants of radicalism's promise. The much-feared anarchist Johann Most, "apostle of terror" to the American yellow press and police, was known better in his own circles as "the Rabelais of the Proletariat." (Only one joke comes down to us: What is the difference, Most asked, between the stockmarket and the toilet? On the stockmarket, the paper falls *before* the crash.) Morris Winchevsky, the *zeyde* [grandfather] of Yiddish Socialist journalism in Europe, arrived in the New York of the 1890s already a literary hero for his popular satire columns "The Crazy Philosopher"—and proceeded to drive philistine socialists as well as Jewish conservatives crazier with his wit. Many now-forgotten figures also knew how to hold a foreign-born audience together with a quick jest. American radical humor magazines appeared in German, Yiddish and even the Finnish language before English, and had more luck sustaining publication.

Home-grown and immigrant radical jokesters had many differences, but one common object. By the 1870s-90s, they faced an official America at its self-congratulatory apex, bloated with moral vindication at the late crusade against slavery yet curiously indifferent to the degradation of the working classes under the spreading industrial-financial empire—and purblind to the change of America's international role from eighteenth century republican champion to twentieth century policeman of property rights. Business and its apologists flatly aimed to keep the impoverished minions in check through star-spangled rhetoric and outright appeals to xenophobia, racism and patriarchy. On the surface, they appeared to succeed. Radicalism disappeared from two-party politics after 1870. Radical Reconstruction drowned in blood and cynicism, reform-minded labor found itself betrayed by its leaders or crushed by unprecedented use of military force, and even mighty Populism was swallowed up by the Democratic Party. Public credulity seemed at times boundless in depth and endless in duration. Radical—and not only radical—humorists set to work puncturing the gassy balloon of national hubris.

American history and its abuses offered orchestrated patriotism an especially convenient tool for deception, but also an ideal target for vengeful satire. Claims to an exceptional history, free of significant conflict and any European- or Asian-style oppression, poured off the presses toward the end of the nineteenth century. "Frontier" theories, racial theories, apologies of every kind and shape found ready praise in the commercial press and the academy. Humorists turned the picture around. "It seems in America they are always boasting of their dead heroes," complains Morris Winchevsky's immigrant Heikl. "They don't have any live ones," concludes the mordant street-philosopher Michael. J.A. Wayland, king of the grassroots radical journalists, added a like-minded jab to wake up his readers: "People don't have titles in America. 'Gin the law, you know. Titled people make people work to keep 'em in luxury, you know, and Americans would never stand for that. No Sirree! Not while the Declaration is read every Fourth, and the name of Lexington, Bunker Hill, Homestead and Coeur d'Alene [two sites of contemporary class warfare] are remembered! No oppression in America, if you please. We are free, we are a great people. The American eagle soars—wonder if it isn't sore."

By the 1890s, the writing of satirical history had become a fine art. Edgar Wilson Nye ("Bill Nye"), a popular lecture-circuit performer and acclaimed literary comedian, surpassed all his previous fame with the *Comic History of the U.S.*, illustrated by the great cartoonist Frederick Burr Opper. Eugene Debs, in his pre-socialist days a dear friend of Nye's, remarked that "beneath his flow of humor there was a sub-stratum of serious meditation. He was the master of pathos as well as the lord of laughter," a more penetrating observer of contemporary society than the official pundits. Bitterly satirical of European class society, Nye also savaged Puritan intolerance, patriotic hero-worshipping ("It is said that Washington had no library, which accounted for his originality") and above all the glamour of war ("Men will fight until it is educated out of them, just as they will no doubt retain rudimentary tails and live in trees till they know better," or again, "Most great wars are arranged by people who stay at home and sell groceries to the widow and orphan and old maids at one hundred per cent advance"). Like nearly all other mainstream literary comics, Nye treated Indians and blacks as victims at best, and he had a thorough misunderstanding of labor radicals. (He labeled Illinois' foreign-born Governor John Peter Altgeld an "amateur American" for his pardoning of the two surviving Haymarket martyrs). Still, for his age, Nye had done the remarkable work of a popular historical iconoclast. Socialists had to learn to do better.

The task fell to Ameringer by default. After a return to Germany, Ameringer re-emerged in the 1890s a prominent lieutenant of Sam "Golden Rule" Jones' Ohio civic reformism, a little later editor of a Columbus labor newspaper, then itinerant organizer for the Brewery Workers and at last a socialist agitator. In those years of supreme socialist confidence at the prospective education of the working class into radicalism, Ameringer shone like a polished stone. "I have seen him in Milwaukee and Chicago," his younger friend Carl Sandburg later testified,

> *taking the platform in a crowded, smoke-filled hall, facing crowds of somber and sober-faced workingmen, talking to them about their troubles, about woe and injustice and inequalities, drawing contrasts, soon bringing smiles to the faces and finally roars of laughter.*

Ameringer had a special skill in delivering the message to the Twainesque society of the southwest, where tenant farmers faced the ultimate last frontier of illusion in their American legacy, and turned sharply to the Left. He played keenly upon the tension between the ideal and reality, winning vast throngs at the socialist "tent meetings" where he and his sons constituted a four-piece musical orchestra. A few other non-humorous socialists, notably A.M. Simons, had already provided extensive historical material for use by socialist lecturers in these extravaganzas and in the rapidly expanding socialist press. Study classes by the thousands sprang up to get the "real story" of America. But something more was needed for the plain reader inclined to be skeptical at patriotic boasts yet unconvinced by socialist arguments. More than anyone else, Ameringer had learned to appreciate the common-sense psychology with its limitations and potentialities. *Life and Deeds of Uncle Sam* was a made-to-order literary creation.

The booklet's original (1909) publication arrived at a most propitious political moment. Much of the earlier rosy optimism about social conditions had already faded. Muckraking popular magazines broadcast details of political corruption and monopoly mismanagement. A "scientific" school of American historians, not socialist but critical of unregulated capitalism, began an era of studied debunking when the educated classes greeted Charles A. Beard's *Economic Interpretation of the Constitution* (1913) as the last word in exposing the none-too-idealistic motives of the Founding Fathers. Meanwhile, widening class conflict and the evident approach of world war fed a popular discontent. Claims of industrial magnates to represent the real America against embattled immigrant textile workers, or to justify the unconstitutional violence on behalf of Rockefeller interests against heroic western miners now rang empty. Ameringer seized the moment with a singularly different version of America in a form the least sophisticated reader could understand.

Life and Deeds of Uncle Sam sold like wildfire, half a million copies before 1917, translation into some fifteen languages (including English: an overeager translator from the German neglected to notice the American original), and a continuing appeal that sparked a 1930s version that was still circulating after Ameringer's death in 1943. This militant manifesto achieved a readership comparable to any best-selling book today. How did Ameringer's work attain this circulation without the fanfare of prestige reviews, movie versions and television talk-shows? We might well ask.

Much of the truth can be found in the spontaneous political enthusiasm *Life and Deeds* generated. No other radical book until, perhaps, *The Autobiography of Malcolm X* was likely so often to be given away by friend to friend or friend to acquaintance in hopes of breaking through politically on some emotional/intellectual level. Like the *Autobiography*, it threw a flashlight upon a different America uncomfortably vivid to any but the willfully blind. It revealed the character of the author as bold, revolutionary, unimpeachably the product of a common culture. And it glistened with superb writing.

Alas! There is another parallel between the unlikely counterparts. Each book appeared as radicalism streaked over the horizon apparently *en route* to oblivion. The daring of the texts predicted the authors' own eclipse. Malcolm went to his early grave the victim of an assassin's bullet, very likely the target of an official conspiracy to crush black rebellion. Ameringer survived the milder repression of free speech and assembly which dogged his near-successful 1916 campaign for Congress on a socialist anti-war platform. But *Life and Deeds* proved his high point after all. The division of the Left in 1919 thrust the great propagandist to the political sidelines. Ameringer toiled in the 1920s as editor of the *Illinois Miner* and in the 1930s of his own *American Guardian*, filling the columns of both papers with his infectious good spirit and his biting attack against capitalism. He became the voice of an older-generation radical America in spiritual exile—until his principled opposition to the coming Second World War silenced his public expression. Although his charming autobiography attracted much attention at its original 1940 publication, neither Communists, Trotskyists or the subsequent New Left had much use for the old man's legacy, and the very memory of him seemed to perish.

The faults readily apparent in *Life and Deeds* long kept the book in a sort of radical purgatory, too important to ignore entirely but almost embarrassing to consider at close range. James R. Green's important historical monograph, *Grass-Roots Socialism* (1978) casts new light on the subject, restoring Ameringer's reputation against his own historical blindspots and his occasionally ill-conceived ethnic humor. Modern readers of *Life and Deeds*, troubled by Ameringer's use of the word "nigger" should know that he played a prominent role in socialist counterattacks against the "Grandfather Clause" intended to exclude blacks from Oklahoma voting rolls, and that he virtually led the struggle against the region's Ku Klux Klan, at considerable risk to himself. Likewise, his use of "kike" and "wop," offensive to our ears, must be understood as part of a freewheeling stage-and-literary humor of the era probably no more prejudiced than our own in this respect, but less cautious in its phraseology. In any case, the foreign-born worker had no prouder political champion. Ameringer's stubborn unwillingness to see a radical component in the Revolutionary War reflects not only uncritical acceptance of the contemporary debunking scholarship but also a plain absence of the evidence historians have uncovered in recent times about "Jack Tar," the archetypal revolutionary sailor whose direct action did much to precipitate the conflict. Ameringer's ignorance of the black role in the Abolitionist movement, the slaves' own decisive struggle in the Civil War and Reconstruction South, is of a piece. Until W.E.B. Dubois' *Black Reconstruction* (1935) even the most radical historians remained blind to the facts. Long did a prejudice against the Abolitionist as catspaw of advancing capitalism reign among iconoclasts, and it has not to this day been overcome. Ameringer felt, in his historical ignorance and his philosophical resolve, that he could not give an inch to past American democracy without compromising the pure negativity of his message. Today, three-quarters of a century later, radical historians are still seeking an elusive balance between the hypocrisy they uncover and the radical democratic ideals that various sectors of society continue to make their own.

Ameringer taught them *how* rather than *what* to write, and it is in his winning style more than his factual acuity that the lasting value of *Life and Deeds* can be found. Ameringer the stage performer and literary artist developed the techniques of the American comic to the utmost. Like rural wits from the archetypal "Down East" Yankee Seba Smith ("Jack Downing") onward, Ameringer perfected the understatement. ("As a shining example of what a war ought to be, the Thirty Years' War is a model that all lovers of war should pattern after.") Like the "Old Southwest" frontier humor of the 1830s which set the tone for Mark Twain and others, Ameringer counterposed to this mechanism its opposite, the exaggeration. (The Puritans "held a prayer meeting to thank the Lord for deliverance from the perils of the wild wave. Next day they caught a Quaker and burned a hole through his tongue. . . ."). The comic reversal, the anti-climax, accent humor: All the minor methods he pulled from his bag of tricks. We can almost imagine Ameringer on the platform, acting out his part like Artemus Ward or Mark Twain, affecting a folksy simple-mindedness and apparent lack of awareness at the phrases that caused his audience to burst out in laughter and cheers. Unlike these home-grown stage comedians and like his fellow immigrant radical jokesters, he added in undisguised workingclass jabs, brought the political pressure to the boiling point until red hilarity inspired wish and optimistic hope for the revenge of history's repressed. Ameringer, the artist-turned-politico, had found a way to bring his talent onto the broadest stage. Like other great humorists, his most fantastic creation was himself.

Paul Buhle

Social Humor Archives
Tamiment Library, New York University
November 1984

Economic Determinism

If you are just an ordinary mortal then you don't know what "economic determinism" is. Well, it isn't part of a steam turbine. Neither is it a poison they put in medicine. It's got nothing to do with algebra or any other thing where they put an X or O or H before or after something which you can't make out. Only scientific men, like myself, know what it is. It's mighty lucky you ran across this little book; otherwise you might have heard the term a thousand times without knowing any more about it than an American statesman. Economic Determinism, brother, is the thing that makes people turn their noses in the direction whence they hear the jingle of easy money. There, now you've got it.

Great masses of people are not set in motion in a given direction just because somebody don't like their religion. Wars and revolutions are not fought because some folks would rather have a red and blue than a black and white flag. Way down at the bottom of every human movement are the selfish material interests of classes which strive against other classes in an endeavor to make an easier living. Now the easiest way to get a living is to get someone to get it for you. Hence men struggle continuously to make others work for them, or to throw off the yoke of those they work for. This struggle is called the class struggle.

When somebody talks about carrying the cross, the flag, freedom, or civilization to some heathen nation you bet your bottom boots that that heathen nation has got something the other fellow wants.

Once a little Jewish boy was fighting with a couple of street urchins on the sidewalk in front of his father's store. When the old man noticed the scrap he yelled, "Quit dat fighting, Ikey." "I can't daddy," shouted back the struggling warrior, "they called me a sheeney."

"Nebber mind vot dey call you, you was a fool to take dot beating," replied old Aaron. "I can't quit, they said I was a Christkiller," yelled Ikey between blows. "Vot you care vot they say you vos," shouted the old man.

"But daddy, I can't quit, I've got my foot on a nickel," came from Ikey's swollen lips.

That nickel under Ikey's foot was the basic cause of the war between him and other kids. And all the gab about sheeney and Christkiller, and being insulted, was only the ideal expression of a material interest.

It's the same thing with the big boys whom we grown-ups call great men. When these folks talk about fighting for justice, eternal right, glory, the flag, God, fatherland or avenging an insult to the nation, watch out for the nickel under the foot. It's there every time and when you understand this you also understand what is meant by the term "Economic Determinism."

Early American History

America was discovered accidentally by a foreigner named Columbus, who was looking for a route to India. He didn't know it was America he had discovered, and the natives understood too little about geography to inform him that he had stumbled into a new world. So when he asked them if this was India and they the Indians, they said, "sure Mike" and the name stuck to them ever since.

One of my ancestors Amergio (Italian) Americus (Latin) Ameringer (German) thought that his name was just about the right thing for the new world and he slapped it on without asking anybody whether it suited them or not. Thus it came about that the natives of America are called Indians, while the foreigners who settled in their country call themselves Americans.

Why People Migrated to America

THE GERMANS

No self-respecting man will admit that he comes from poor stock or that he left his native heath because there weren't enough eating apples on the family tree. Hence, most of the poor folks who came to America emigrated, ostensibly to escape religious persecution.

It cannot be denied, however, that religious persecution did its fair share in those days to make people seek peace and eatables among the heathen in the American wilderness.

Germany just then had gone through a religious war that lasted thirty years. The question under discussion was, "Shall priests and nobles together rob the working people, or shall the nobles do the job alone?" When the religious (?) controversy was ended, Germany was a howling wilderness. More people got killed, were starved to death and died during epidemics than in any other war before or after. As a shining example of what a war really ought to be, the Thirty Years' war is the model that all lovers of war should pattern after. The Protestant armies cut down the fruit trees, drove off the cattle, and burned down the homes of Catholics and the Catholic army did the same things for the Protestants. When pious people kill each other for Christ's sake, it is only natural that innocent bystanders should get hurt.

The population of Germany shrank from sixteen to four million. Cannibalism reappeared. The gallows had to be guarded to prevent the starving people from devouring the corpses dangling from the ropes. Mothers had to be watched to keep them from eating their newborn babies. Where thriving towns had been, herds of wild wolves roamed unmolested. The survivors appeased their hunger on grass, roots, leaves and bodies stolen from the graveyards. Taken all in all, it was a glorious war and should serve as an everlasting inspiration to the upholders of militarism.

Degraded, brutalized and poverty stricken, the miserable Germans fled from devastated fields and burning homes down the Rhine to Amsterdam where they sold themselves to ship captains for the price of a passage to the new world. Thus the spiritual and worldly rulers drove the people from the German fatherland.

THE SCOTCH-IRISH

The next big batch of immigrants came from Ireland —the Scotch-Irish. These people had built up a flourishing industry in the weaving of wool. Their product came in competition with the woolen goods turned out by English manufacturers. The English capitalists claimed that they could not compete against the "pauper labor product" of Ireland. But instead of asking, like gentlemen or American capitalists, for a protective tariff in order to destroy their competitors, they evoked the British Parliament to pass measures to close the Irish looms altogether. When this demand was granted in 1698, tens of thousands of the Protestant weavers of Ulster deserted their idle looms and came to America.

THE PLAIN IRISH

Under feudalism the land belonged to the Lord and the serfs belonged to the land. When the nobles sold their land, the serfs went with it as part of the improvement. At times, when there was no work to be done in the fields of his Lordship, the serfs could work for themselves in order to procure sufficient grub and rags to keep alive and clothed until the bell on the castle called them to work for the Lord again. The poor devils didn't get much of a living out of the game, but even the little they got was more than "His Grace," the Lord, was willing to give. So when the raising of wool became a paying proposition, the nobility and many of the monasteries turned their land over to the sheep.

The dear little sheep didn't need expensive straw-thatched huts to live in. They were not spoiled by eating bread made of good bran. No rags were necessary to keep them warm. On the contrary, they raised more all-wool suits on their bodies than they had use for. Sheep haven't got much of a reputation for being fighters, but they chased a whole lot of people out of Ireland, who years afterwards, as full-fledged cops, chased other poor devils off the grass in Central Park, New York.

THE PURITANS

The largest consignment of Englishmen ever loaded on a single ship came over in the Mayflower. In fact, nearly everybody that is anybody in America is a descendant of one of the multitude of first cabin passengers of the Mayflower. No modern ocean greyhound could hold one-tenth of the people that populated the above ark on its turbulent voyage to the land of the free and the home of the brave.

The Puritans were Protestant, middleclass people, who had gotten a little the worst of it in their scrap with the Catholic cavaliers. Being unable to persecute others on account of their religious belief, they skipped out to escape religious persecution themselves.

After landing at Plymouth Rock they held a prayer meeting to thank the Lord for deliverance from the perils of the wild wave. Next day they caught a Quaker and burned a hole through his tongue because he prayed to the wrong God or to the right God in the wrong way, I have forgotten which.

The Puritans were a pious, bigoted and intolerant lot who regarded a chronic spell of "blues" as the natural state of man and who embodied their vinegar ideas into a set of laws called "blue laws."

When a Puritan was caught telling a joke he was soaked in salt water and then buried alive under a weeping willow, while the sinner who laughed at the joke was roasted to death first and buried in unhallowed ground afterwards. Witchburning was their only amusement and when other folks put a stop to this practice, the Puritans invented the Thanksgiving dinner and got even. Nine-tenths of the good things told about the Puritans are lies and the remaining tenth isn't quite true.

Not all of the English Puritans ran away to America to escape religious persecution. Those who had sand enough remained in the Mother country and fought it out with the Cavaliers like men. When, under the leadership of Cromwell, the latter were finally beaten to a standstill, it was their turn to skedaddle in order to escape persecution on account of their theological views and convictions.

The Pilgrim fathers had settled in New England and the Cavaliers, not wishing to annoy them in their new homes, settled as far south as the lay of the land would permit.

White Slavery

I know a man who at one time in his life had a boil on his body. I have forgotten the exact place the boil was located, but at any rate it made him sleep on his stomach. The boil disappeared long ago, but the man still sleeps in that position. He never got over it. The cause is gone but the habit remains. So it was with the working people who in early days came to this country. They had worked for Lords, Priests and Capitalists so long, they had gotten used to it and couldn't get over the habit even under a new environment. I guess they thought it was the natural order of things to have a boss.

And there were lots of people willing to boss them.

People who fight the struggle for existence through substitutes are called "the better class." Some of that kind also landed on our inhospitable shore and proceeded to hog the land along the rivers. Not only is river bottom land the most productive, but the river also furnishes a means of transportation. Those who couldn't get land worked for those who did get it, and a new feudalism sprang up; this new feudalism looked as much like the European article as one egg looks like another.

There was plenty of land; only when a fellow got too far away from the settlement, he was liable to leave his locks with an Indian hairdresser who used a butcher knife for a hair-cut. On one side was the ocean and on the other side the Indians, and the land between the two was gobbled up by court favorites, merchants and adventurers.

The land-owners bought the poor immigrants from the ship companies and set them to work on their plantations. When they couldn't get enough voluntary immigrants, they got their agents to steal children in English cities.

Another class of involuntary immigrants were the criminals and prostitutes sent over by the English authorities. But these people either died on the passage over, or soon after landing, for I never have heard of a single man whose ancestors were condemned to emigrate.

Whenever a shipload of immigrants was landed, the buyers of white slaves flocked to the harbor to pick out bargains. Sometimes not all could be disposed of in the seaport so the remainder were turned over to agents who chained them together and peddled them from town to town.

So you see there's no use being so all fired up because you came from one of the oldest American families. Maybe the founder of your house entered Boston on the tail end of a log chain with a sign hung around his neck saying "Last of a job lot. Marked down from $25.00 to $19.98." Or maybe your great, great, great, great, great grandmother, the one you mention as the colonial Grand Dame, was purchased by a Jamestown bachelor, for a bale of frostbitten tobacco. The tobacco was a little damaged, but so was the lady, and a fair exchange is not cheating.

The exploiting class, here as everywhere, formed only an insignificant minority of the population. But the white slaves and indentured servants had all the spunk taken out of them in the old country, so they just laid on their stomachs and let the few walk over them.

The Ruling Class in Colonial Times

The aristocracy of colonial days was composed of a motley aggregation of feudal lords, adventurers, busted nobles, slave-traders, smugglers, slave-owners and merchants. All these elements had but one thing in common, namely, to get rich without working.

The English and Dutch governments, anxious to have their colonies settled, gave liberal land grants to people who founded settlements or plantations. Adventurers who shanghaied, kidnapped or persuaded fifty working people to the new land were usually given sixteen miles of land on one side of a navigable river. The whole state of New Hampshire at one time belonged to one man. In many cases these land grants were obtained from the royal governors by the liberal application of bribe money. Under liberal bribes we must not understand the fabulous sums paid in our own times by Senatorial candidates to Legislative representatives. A hundred dollars handed to the right party would often bring to the donor a principality of the size of Rhode Island.

These new country feudal lords called themselves patroons, a name that most likely arose from the fact that they patronized the laboring people who kept them in luxury and idleness.

The patroons organized their colonies in royal style. Many kept up small armies of retainers and cut-throats. They held court and fought and plundered under their own banner. The colonists paid rent for the use of the land. Besides this, nearly every paying industry was declared a monopoly of the patroon. Most everything needed by the actual settlers had to be bought from the patroons and if the settlers had anything to sell the patroon saw to it that he was the only buyer in sight. The wealth-producers in colonial days suffered nearly as much from oppressive monopolies as they do nowadays.

The Slave Traders

In the year of our Lord 1662, "The Company of Royal Adventurers Trading to Africa" was chartered by his Christian majesty Charles II, by the grace of God, defender of the faith, etc. The dowager queen and the duke of York were let in on the ground floor. The purpose of the company was to supply the West Indies with 3000 African slaves annually. For some reason the scheme failed and the company sold its charter in 1672 to the "Royal African Company" organized for the same purpose by the same Charles II.

In 1692 the British Parliament cut into the monopoly of his royal nibs by allowing English merchants to trade in African slaves, provided they paid ten percent duty on goods exported to Africa. American merchants, seeing a good thing, soon clamored for the privilege to participate in the noble trade. Among those who hollered the loudest to be let in were the liberty-loving, God-fearing Puritans of the New England states. Their wish was granted and gentlemen who dealt in "black ivory" became numerous in the northern seaport towns. Soon the slave-traders rose to rank and position. "Money stink," says the Frenchman, not even when it is in the slave traffic. From the influence exerted by ave-trader in church and state we may justly conclude that he was of as much importance as the franchise-grabbing, council-corrupting and legislature-bribing leading citizen of our own times. That the slave-trader sat in the front pew in church, lectured before the Y.M.C.A. (if there was one), and was interviewed on every question from hookworms to astronomy goes without saying. He was the real thing and woe unto him who reflected on the angelic purity of his calling. True, it appears that no one ever ventured such a preposterous thing, excepting possibly a few German Quakers. But these were ignorant foreigners totally bereft of all understanding of American institutions.

Slavery was never a paying propositton in the northern colonies and this fact permitted an early recognition of the ungodliness of the institution. But while there was no money in slavery there was plenty of it in the slave trade. It is therefore only natural that we should find condemnation of slavery and approbation of the slave traffic going harmoniously together.

When our God-fearing ancestors imported the black heathens they didn't do so because they had a grudge against them. It was purely a matter of business. They tried to work Indians on their plantations first but these, being a kind of rudimentary aristocrats themselves, rather died than worked.

And just as slavery came in as a matter of business, it went out the same way. It was finally abolished because the black slave constituted the breadbasket of the Confederate army. To destroy the latter, slavery was abolished.

The Smugglers

Many of the thrifty New England shipowners engaged in the smuggling of tea. There was an export and an import duty on this article. The American smugglers, by landing their cargoes at out-of-the-way places in the dark, saved themselves at least the import duty. This allowed them to sell tea cheaper than the English merchants who were foolish enough to pay both duties. English tea accumulated in Boston harbor. When finally the English Parliament rebated the export duty to the British traders, allowing them to sell their product as cheap as the American smugglers, the smugglers got busy and threw the English tea into the Boston Harbor.

This version of the Boston tea party is not quite as inspiring as the one taught in schools, but whatever it may lack in inspiration it makes up in truthfulness.

John Hancock who signed his name so boldly under the Declaration of Independence was then called the King of Smugglers. On the day when the battle of Lexington was fought he was to appear before the Admirality Court of Boston along with his lawyer, John Adams. Mr. Hancock was accused of having robbed the government of England of $500,000 in import duties. Now you understand why some of these patriots said, "We must all hang together, else they'll hang us all separately."

Causes of the Revolutionary War

If you seek for the cause of the "War for Independence" don't look into little Mary's school history. It isn't there. These school histories are fairytales with the "Once upon a time" cut out and dates inserted instead.

The cause of the revolutionary war, as of every war, revolution, rebellion, reformation, crusade or upheaval is the same cause that made little Ikey fight: the nickel under the foot.

Mary's book tells about great men who held a meeting in Philadelphia about 1774 and decided that "all men are born free and equal, with rights to life, liberty, and the pursuit of happiness." One patriot got up and said, "I make a motion that all governments derive their just power from the consent of the governed." Everybody shouted "Ay!" The next fellow arises and said, "I move there shall be no taxation without representation." This is adopted with a whoop. Then a fellow who had kissed the blarney stone on all four sides climbs on the table and thunders, "Give me liberty or give me death!" That settled it. The revolutionary war was started.

But Mary's book said nothing about the nickel under the foot.

What were these great men fussing about? What had the dear old mother country done to make them so huffy?

Well, the mother country had levied a tax on tea. Ahem, that's more like it. Now we're getting down to business.

The mother country had slapped a stamp tax on notes, bonds, stocks, wills, testaments, etc.

Keep it up, we'll soon get somewhere. What else?

They taxed rum and molasses—Well, I swan!

The English Parliament discouraged our manufacture and commerce.

You don't say!

American citizens had been yanked before English admiralty courts and thrown into British prisons.

What for?

Smuggling.

Now we demand trials before courts of our own and by juries of our peers. Why so?

To keep out of jail.

The English government won't accept the nice paper money we print ourselves. What a shame.

Well, we have struck rock bottom at last. These patriots were members of a property-owning class. Like all property-owners they had it in for the tax-collector. They wanted good American dollars to stay in their own pockets. Interfering with the sacred privilege of making profits was another violation of the laws of God and man. Laws were fine things to keep the lower classes in check. But when the law goes so far as to affect the pocketbooks of the very best citizens then it is high time to call a halt.

Now do you see the nickel under the foot?

Easy enough, but what's all this talk about equal rights, rights of man, government of the people, for the people, eternal rights, justice, liberty, freedom, etc.?

Oh! That's the ideal superstructure arising above the basis of economic interests. That fine talk was to rile up those who didn't have a nickel to stand on.

The Working People of 1774

The workers of that period were not affected by the causes that made their masters rebel against English rule. The tax on tea should have left them cool as a cucumber, for the simple reason that the free workers were too poor to drink tea, and the slaves and indentured servants didn't get any. Tea in those days was about as expensive as champagne and Rhine wine is today. When the working people drank tea it was sassafras tea and there was no tax on that kind.

It was the same with the stamp tax. Working people who possessed valuable paper requiring stamps to be pasted on, a hundred and forty years ago, were as scarce as hen's teeth.

The tax on rum and molasses was not on the rum and molasses consumed in the homes of the workers, but on the rum and molasses used in the African slave trade. The trade in "black ivory' was one of the leading industries of the colonies. And the very best people engaged in it. They used to buy molasses in the West Indies, take it up to Connecticut and convert it into rum. Then they shipped the booze to Africa and swapped it for slaves. The slaves were taken to the West Indies, exchanged for molasses and the molasses was taken to Connecticut. Well, I could keep it up all day. It was kind of a sorry-go-round of "molasses, rum and niggers." The English ruling class at one time had a monopoly on this trade and thought it was still entitled to a "dip-in," after the American slave-traders had taken over the industry. Hence the tax on rum and molasses.

"No Taxation without Representation" is a mighty fine thing to talk about, but to save my gizzard, I can't see why the workers of 1774 should have been so unduly excited about that issue. Nearly every colony had disfranchised the workers by means of property qualifications.

Benjamin Franklin told the story of a man in Philadelphia who voted because he owned a mule. One day the mule died and the man lost his vote. And Franklin asked the question, "Was it the man or the mule that voted?" My opinion is, it was the mule, and the more I think about it the more I am convinced that the mule has kept on voting until this very day.

Hurrah for Liberty

Trial by a jury of your peers is another great stunt. Only the propertyless toilers of the revolutionary period got no chance to serve on juries. They were judged by their superiors, mostly without the formality of a jury trial. The slave-owner was the sole judge and master of life and death over his slaves. The feudal lords (patroons) had arrogated to themselves the same rights in regards to their white slaves. And the indentured servant could be beaten, tortured, jailed and starved by his masters without court or jury.

Of all the issues that agitated the colonists there wasn't a single one that affected the working people any more than the freckles on your nose affect the course of Saturn. All of which did not prevent the working people from going to war and fighting like demons for the pocketbooks of their exploiters. It was for this propertyless class and the idealists that all the fine phrases of the Declaration of Independence were written.

Had the masters of 1774 gone to the workers and said, "Here fellows, take these shooting irons, and pepper the redcoats over yonder. If you fight hard enough and win out, we'll save ourselves boodles of money. We won't have to pay that fine of $500,000 for smuggling and will be able to keep the land we swiped in the Ohio valley. When victory is ours we'll let you cut enough wood on the public land to make yourselves wooden legs. You also may get free lodging in our debtors' prison any time you get hard up"—had the masters talked in that strain, the workers most likely would have taken a sneak towards the tall timber, fetching the guns along for souvenirs.

This kind of chin music don't go with us. We need a different gab. But when that bunch of slave-owners, smugglers, capitalists, lawyers and landlords came before us and recited "We take it to be self-evident that all men are born free and equal, with equal rights to life, liberty, and the pursuit of happiness." we threw our greasy caps in the air and shouted, "That's the dope, hurrah for liberty, hurrah for equality, hurrah for the pursuit of happiness! That's the stuff we are after."

Victory

For seven years the toilers fought, starved and froze for their masters. They left the imprints of their bleeding feet at Valley Forge and Yorktown. And when the war was over they found themselves hopelessly in debt to the merchants and the usurers, whose battles they had fought. The returning heroes were thrown into debtors' prisons by the scores. It was the fashion then to lock men up in jail the moment they were so unfortunate as to owe their fellows a sixpence or a shilling.

During the war the Continental Congress had issued paper money. This currency was called continental script. Hence the phrase "not worth a continental." The soldier in the field received his pay in continental script. So did the farmers who furnished hogs, cattle, wheat, and corn to the army. The money had depreciated until it was worth about ten cents on the dollar. Every time these patriotic soldiers and farmers received a paper dollar from the government they could exchange it for a dime's worth of goods.

Now money don't stick to the hands of the poor people. It would have to be printed on fly paper or have barbs on the edges to do that. Gradually the continental script had gravitated towards the strong boxes of the merchants and users. When the bloody war was over, these gentlemen blandly asked the people to whom they had paid dimes for dollars, to pay them dollars for dimes.

Of course they didn't put it that way. You can't catch flies with vinegar. So the money sharks called out the hot-air artists and embryo Fourth-of-July spielers whose I.O.U.'s they held and told them to go to it. Whereupon this gentry climbed the rostrums and elocuted something like this: "Surely this young and glorious nation will not enter the stage of history by repudiating its honest debts. Surely the men who have bled and died that liberty may live, who have fought under the sacred folds of the palladium of freedom fluttering in the winds of justice, kissed by the smiling rays of the golden sun in the shades of the giant pinions of the American eagle who floats majestically over the land of the free and the home of the brave, surely the men who have laid down their lives as a libation on the altars of their country are not the kind to rob poor widows and orphans of their hard-earned savings. Is there a man within the sound of my voice so base, etc., etc.,?''

That's the kind of dope to sling at the horny-handed sons of toil. They take to it like puppies take to milk. What? Rob widows and orphans? I should say not. We've been there too often and know how it feels. Show us the fellow who wants to rob widders and orphans. Well, there was one.

Shays' Rebellion

The plutes of Massachusetts tried to collect five million dollars from 90,000 bankrupt farmers by means of the poll tax.

This is the meanest tax ever invented. It makes men like Rockefeller and blind beggars pay the same amount. The hard cash so collected was to be exchanged for the script in the claws of the spectators, dollars for dimes. The farmers didn't see it that way, and under Daniel Shays, a veteran of the Revolutionary War, they arose in armed rebellion.

It had been all right for these ''minute men'' to fight for the dollars of the ruling class, but when they tried to scrap for the dollars in their own pockets the conduct became high treason and the Massachusetts militia was called upon to stamp out the rebellion. There was not money in the state treasury to pay the warriors, whereupon the patriotic merchants and bankers of Boston chipped in and raised the wherewithal. Beats the land how patriotic and liberal some people can get when they see a prospect of getting something for nothing.

Framing the Constitution

The Shays' rebellion and similar risings of debtors in other colonies scared the wits out of the well-to-do's.

In an instant public opinion changed completely. Stern patriots who, while all went well, talked of the dangers of baneful aristocracies, soon learned to talk of the dangers of baneful democracies. Something had to be done to keep the rabble in check.

Revolting had become respectable during the war and the exploited masses "in the pursuit of happiness" might get it into their heads to shake the domestic exploiters off their own backs even as they had shaken off the foreign exploiters from the backs of their masters. A strong central government was necessary to collect debts, public and private. Besides this the manufacturers were clamoring for a protective tariff for their "infant industries."

The farmers and wage-workers who had never gotten anything from this or any other government were opposed to a central government. But nobody cared what they wanted or didn't want.

The first step towards a new government came from George Washington. George, it is said, couldn't tell a lie, but since he was a planter, and not a retail dealer or lawyer, this failing did not prevent him from becoming the richest man in the colonies. He invited a couple of gentlemen to his Mt. Vernon home to talk things over. Having done so, they invited more of their kind to meet at a commercial convention at Annapolis on September 11, 1789. This convention asked the Continental Congress to issue a call for another meeting. And in February 1787, this body passed a resolution, saying that it was expedient that a convention of delegates from the several states be held in Philadelphia in May for the sole purpose of revising the Articles of Confederation and report back to Congress. The resolution didn't say anything about framing a constitution or adopting a new form of government.

Pursuant to this resolve the colonies sent their delegates to the city of brotherly love. Mary's little history lets on as if these delegates were elected by the sovereign American voting kings. That isn't true. They were picked by the legislatures and represented not all of the people, but only some of them and a precious some at that. Who came? Slave-owners and their lawyers from the south, merchants, bankers, ship-owners, landlords and their lawyers from the north. There were two workingmen in the crowd. One of them was Benjamin Franklin who was eighty-two years old by that time. Sixty years before, he had been a printer. In the meantime he had become postmaster general of the colonies, was the owner of the largest publishing house and had acted for some years as the business agent of the colonial property owners at the court of England.

The other was Roger Sherman. Once upon a time a shoemaker, but he got converted before it was too late and became a rich lawyer. Besides these two horny-handed representatives of the toiling masses there were four farmers. At least they said they were. Their biographers added the information that they were graduates of Yale and had been in England to receive the finishing touches to their education. From this we may conclude that they were never kicked off the milk stool by a fly-bitten brindle cow.

From all we can find out, the first few days of the Convention were taken up with such *precautious* remarks as "psst, keep mum; not a word; this is on the q.t., not so loud, somebody will hear," etc. After that, the fathers of the constitution closed the doors, pulled down the blinds, chased the cat out and hung hats over the keyholes. What went on on the inside is not precisely known, as the delegates were pledged to secrecy and were not permitted to make copies of the minutes. One of them, James Madison, made private notes and from these it can be gathered that the fathers on the inside concocted some kind of a practical joke on the people on the outside. The joke as it turned out afterwards was the Constitution of the United States.

So much punk has been written about "the American Form of Government," "the most monumental document ever devised by the wisdom of men," and so many high-school graduates, Thanksgiving-day orators, and Fourth-of-July spielers have slobbered over the venerable old document, that I feel it my sacred duty to shed some much-needed light on the subject.

Our Undemocratic Democracy

Constitutional governments arose from a desire of the many to curb the ruling power of the sovereign.

The king in olden times was lawmaker, chief executive, supreme court, and tax-assessor, all wrapped in one bundle. He was also the principal real-estate owner of the land, deriving his title from God himself. Besides this he was the defender of the *then existing* only true faith. The partnership between the Almighty and his royal highness was satisfactory as far as the two contracting parties were concerned. It gave to the king the material for a happy earthly existence, while he used his high commission to keep his benighted subjects on the straight and narrow path to heaven. The king had a "good thing," but it is one of the characteristics of wicked human nature to demand that a good thing should be passed around. The first people to desire to curb the power of the king were the nobles and priests. These gentle folks composed his majesty's spiritual and bodily police force. Without them he could not rule. In those days the constitutional struggle was between king and aristocracy. The monarch was striving to make his authority supreme while the nobles sought to curtail and limit it.

During the reign of King John of England a combination of feudal barons, priests and freemen forced upon this monarch, the *Magna Carta,* the Great Charter. This document is popularly supposed to form the cornerstone of England's freedom. But precious little freedom did it contain for the masses. The nobility, clergy, and freemen it benefited formed but an insignificant small minority of the population. The masses were not affected by the great charter which conferred the governmental power from the one to the few.

From now on nobility and clergy shared in the power of the monarch. The great council composed of the aristocracy became a constitutional check on the power of the king. The first job taken from his majesty was that of tax assessor. Without the consent of the great council he could not levy taxes.

By and by the great council split into two separate bodies, the House of Lords, composed of the top-notchers among the priests and nobles, and the House of Commons, representing the rising capitalist class.

The troubles of the king multiplied and the government became a three-cornered affair. Each division became a check on the other two. The king couldn't make a move without the consent of the lords, the lords couldn't budge without permission of the commons, and lords and commons couldn't do a thing without the sanction of the king. Each party was fighting for more power and in the end the king lost the right to levy taxes entirely. Later on the law-making power was taken from the king and still later he even lost the right to veto the actions of Parliament.

The one man's power was effectively done away with.

The sovereign monarch became a figurehead and England was ruled by the House of Lords composed of the land-owning nobility, the dignitaries of the church, and the House of Commons made up of the commercial and industrial interests.

The essential fact in the development of constitutional government is the rise to political power of classes which compete with the king and with each other for the control of the state.

Under this form of government the different governing bodies act as checks upon each other. Each one may veto the acts of the other two and since the unanimous consent of all three is required for the enaction of laws, a small minority can block legislation. In this manner it may force the majority to recognize its demands.

The majority of the people are supposed to rule in a democracy. Instead of a sovereign king we have the sovereign people. The struggle for political power enters into a new stage. As a minority of aristocrats at one time curbed the powers of the sovereign king so a new minority composed of the wealthy class seeks *to curb and check the power of "the sovereign people."*

The American Government a Foreign Import

At the time the Constitution was framed, England had a government of three heads.

King.

House of Lords.

House of Commons.

His majesty had already lost the veto power and the right to appoint judges. Even the House of Lords was not the influential body it once was. The dominant power rested in the House of Commons and the boss of the strongest political party in the lower house was practically the uncrowned king of England. His official title was "Prime Minister." This form of government was imported and, after a backward revision, adopted by the framers of the Constitution.

First the fathers brought the House of Commons over here and changed the name into House of Representatives. The people should rule not directly, but through representatives, chosen by them. Congress is elected by the people and accountable to the people. If we don't like the record of a Congressman we have the power to oust him when his term is over. A single representative body, responsible to the voters, is easily influenced by the will of the masses. But in the opinion of the aristocratic gentlemen who framed the constitution, "rule of the people" was a very undesirable thing.

Therefore they imported the House of Lords and called it the Senate of the United States. Unfortunately we had no hereditary nobility to choose from, so instead of getting plain Lords for the job they selected landlords.

Senators were not to be elected by the people, but were to be chosen by the legislatures of the different states. In most states the propertyless were disfranchised. Only property-owners could vote and only big property owners could be elected to the legislature. In Massachusetts, for instance, a candidate for the office of governor had to be a Christian *worth five thousand dollars.* This would have shut Jesus Christ out from becoming governor of that state. But these puritans never had a sense of humor nohow. In Virginia the candidate for governor had to be worth ten thousand pounds in sterling. Only men who owned a quarter of an acre of land in towns or twenty-five acres in the country could vote, and only big land-owners and slave-owners were eligible to sit in the legislature.

Now as stated before, the Senate was not to be elected by the sovereign people. Big property-owners elected by little property-owners selected the biggest one to fill the office of United States Senator. *The Senate, not elected by the people*, was created to be a check on the House of Representatives elected by the people.

Next the fathers imported the king himself. Certainly they didn't call him king, but President. But there is nothing in a name. If we would call a polecat an American beauty rose, the interesting animal wouldn't smell any sweeter on account of the change in the name.

The fact is, the Constitution gave to the president a greater power than was possessed by King George the Third of England, against whose tyranny we had revolted. In the first place the president was not to be elected by popular vote. The legislature (always keep in mind the class that sits in these bodies) was to select electors and these in turn would meet in the Electoral College and select the president. This arrangement was later on changed and now the federal office-holders and those wishing to become such, select in convention assembled *two men* from which the dear people may choose. To the president, thus removed from the will of the people, this Constitution gave the veto power over Congress. It also gave him the power to appoint the federal judges and the Supreme Court judges. These judges we must remember are appointed for life by one man and cannot be ousted by the people. They are therefore absolutely free and independent of the will of the sovereign people. In fact they are above the people.

The Supreme Court later on arrogated to itself the power to declare laws passed by Congress "unconstitutional." Certainly the courts never would have dared such an outrageous thing if the fathers and those who succeeded them had not winked both eyes.

A Democracy with Strings Attached

Now let's see what kind of democracy we really got. Democracy means Rule of the People and if it can be shown that the people don't rule in this country then we have no Democracy.

The majority of the sovereign people, let us say, demand a certain law and elect four hundred Congressmen to pass it. Two hundred and one of these gentlemen refuse to vote for the law and it is therefore not passed.

Check number one.

If on the contrary, the majority in the House of Representatives pass the act demanded by the majority of the people, then the bill is referred to the United States Senate. Here are ninety men elected by the legislatures, and not by the people, and for a term of six years—a sufficient length of time to give the dear people a chance to forget. Forty-six out of the ninety senators vote against the bill demanded by a majority of the people. The bill is killed. *Check number two.*

If on the other hand the Senate should pass the bill, then it is up to one man, the president, to say whether it becomes a law or not. If it don't suit him he may veto the act. *Check number three.*

Should the bill pass both houses of Congress and receive the signature of the president, then the Supreme Court has one more whack at it. If five of the nine judges stick their wobbly old corporation lawyer heads together and say "This bill is unconstitutional" that's the end of the poor thing and the ninety odd million voting kings may stand on their heads and flap their long sovereign ears for all the good it may do. *Check number four.*

The fathers said, "Let the people rule," and then went after the people in the following fashion.

The will of ninety million people may be vetoed by two hundred and one members of the House of Representatives.

The will of the House of Representatives may be vetoed by forty-six senators.

The will of the Senate may be vetoed by one man, the president.

And the will of the people and the House of Representatives and the United States Senate and his excellency, the president, may be vetoed by five petrified, musty, old corporation lawyers, who are, as far as popular control is concerned, as far removed from the people, as the man in the moon is removed from the rat-terrier that barks at him.

In monarchies, when the monarch becomes crazy and has to be removed to a padded cell, he retains his royal title, but a prince regent is appointed to sit on the throne and read the typewritten speeches handed to him by the Prime Minister. Well, the fathers of the Constitution persuaded the *sovereign people* that while they were sovereign, all right, they needed a prince regent to do the governing for them. And since we had no thoroughbred princes, they invented the checks of the Senate, the President, and the Supreme Court.

Kings used to claim that they received their power from God himself. The framers of the Constitution couldn't very readily claim the same thing for this document, especially while the writings of Thomas Paine still lingered in the minds of the masses. But in the course of time they succeeded in canonizing the Constitution. What was originally a scheme to rob the people of self-government was praised to the sky until the dense masses accepted the constitutional straitjacket as the ermine of popular sovereignty.

The fathers also wisely provided that the Constitution once accepted, could only be amended with the greatest difficulty. It requires two-thirds of the states to move an amendment and if three-fourths of the states vote favorably on the amendment it goes into force. Hence if a majority in a few of the smallest states vote against the amendment, the will of the overwhelming majority, possibly nine-tenths of the people, is set at naught. That it is not possible in ordinary times to change the Constitution is evident from the fact that, of some twenty-two hundred propositions for amendment, only fifteen have been adopted.

The One Great Paramount Issue

After the exploiters had taken a fall out of the people they fell out among themselves. The bone of contention was the tariff. The South raised tobacco, rice, indigo and cotton. It sold these products mostly in England. The ships that carried the southern agricultural products to the mother country had to return loaded with manufactured articles to make the voyage pay. The South therefore stood for free trade.

During the war, importation from England had practically ceased. The American boycott against English goods put another kink in the English trade. The capitalist method of production sprang up in the north. This method has one characteristic feature, the desire for profit.

Under capitalism, goods are produced for profit. Profits are the difference between the cost of production and the selling price of the products. To produce cheap and sell high is the one great ideal of capitalism. The manner by which goods are produced cheap are low wages, child and woman labor, and machinery. But low wages and high prices are a contradiction. Lower wages also lower the purchasing power of the most numerous class, the wage-workers. This class not only produces all wealth, it is also the principal customer of the capitalist class. *How on earth can people with low wages pay high prices?* For instance, the shoemaker gets one dollar for making a pair of shoes, and the hatmaker gets one dollar for making one hat. If, then, shoes sell for four dollars a pair and hats for four dollars apiece, then the shoemaker must make four pair of shoes before he can buy one hat and the hatmaker must make four hats before he can buy one pair of shoes, while three hats and three pairs of shoes are benevolently assimilated by the capitalist class.

Since the wages of these workers are too low to buy the products of their own labor, the capitalist has three pairs of shoes and three hats left over.

If the products of labor, which the workers cannot buy, accumulate on the shelves of the storekeeper, then this gentleman stops ordering fresh goods. When no orders come in the factory, that place is shut down and the workers are shut out. When the workers are shut out their pay stops and they quit buying altogether and go begging or stealing. This condition is called a panic.

The cause of panics, we are told by the wise men whom an all-wise providence has appointed to do the thinking for us poor devils, is overproduction. Overproduction means that the workers are starving because they raised too much to eat. It means that we go barefooted because we made too many shoes, and we sleep in boxcars and jails because we built too many homes. Overproduction means the same thing as underconsumption, but it sounds better. When a fellow starves to death because he knows there is too much to eat, he dies with an easier conscience.

If the wages of the workers equaled the selling price of their products, then there could be neither overproduction nor underconsumption and this life would form one unbroken chain of prosperity, only interrupted occasionally by hilarious good times. But in this heavenly state there would be no room for capitalists or profits.

Since the capitalists are unwilling to raise the wages of their workers to a point where they can buy the products of their labor, they must find other people than their own employees to buy their goods. If, for instance, the total wages of a given country amount to ten million dollars and the total product is to sell for twenty million dollars then the capitalists must sell ten million dollars worth of goods outside of that country or have a panic on hand. Capitalism must conquer new markets, must ever expand or bust.

The budding American manufacturers had to find a market for the surplus filched from their workers. But they could not sell to England, because the English capitalists produced even cheaper than the American brand. They could not sell to the West, because miserable wagon roads and ox teams made transportation too expensive.

There was but one market to get—the south. American rivers run north and south and furnished a cheap method of transportation. But, as already stated, the south was doing business with England and was unwilling to pay its American confederates a dollar and a half for the same goods that could be bought from England for one dollar.

There was but one way by which the southern market could be gotten. That way was a tariff high enough to shut out English goods. When this was proposed in Congress the south squealed. It has squealed ever since and will squeal for some time to come. But fox-hunting and directing the activity of the slaves through the medium of hired overseers don't put the same sharp edge on men as trading does. The southern slave-owners were no match for the sharp New England traders. The first Congress passed a tariff bill. Every subsequent Congress tinkered with the tariff and put it up a little, or down a little, but mostly up.

The tariff war between the men who make goods and the people who buy goods, between manufacturers and agriculturalists, between north and south, has waged for 130 years. There have been minor issues, such as slavery and money issues, but the one overtowering issue of the last century and a third has been the tariff. What then was the position of the workers on this one great question?

The Workers and the Tariff

In the beginning the advocates of a protective tariff did not claim that it would protect labor. Labor then had no vote. So what was the use to fool it? But as soon as the workers obtained the franchise, free trade and tariff were urged in the interests of the horny-handed sons of toil.

"A high tariff," said the capitalists, "will promote industry; raise wages, and protect the American toilers against the pauper laborers of Europe."

"Free trade," said the slave-owner, "will lower the cost of living and make short wages go a long way."

From all this may be seen that both capitalists and slave-owners were animated by the most unselfish motives. Being of a purely altruistic make-up they placed the welfare of the toilers above their own class interest. How be-auty-fool.

It was easy to divide the ignorant workers on the tariff issue. Somehow the toilers always have great difficulty to make both ends (wages and cost of living) meet. Either wages are too low or the cost of living is too high. Those who wanted wages to catch up with the cost of living joined hands with the capitalist. While the others who wanted the cost of living to come down to their wages made common cause with the slave-owners. But what the poor devils overlooked was the fact that *in the long run and under free competition the wages of the workers are determined by the cost of living*. Where the cost of living is high, wages are high, where living is cheap, wages are low. This is the rule. There are exceptions, but they only prove the rule. Wages follow the cost of living, as the tail follows the kite. They go up and down together, but up or down the workers in the long run will receive just enough wages to keep their bodies and souls together. This thing is called "the iron law of wages." While it is iron all right enough, it may be heated and then bent or hammered into different shapes, but as soon as you quit the heating or hammering, it cools down to hard, inflexible iron again.

More About Wages

Whatever it costs to produce the labor power of the worker, under free competition, will be the wages of the worker in the long run. Labor power is produced with rice, corn, beans, potatoes, kraut, bread, eggs, milk and meat. These things are shoved into the stomach; are burned up and produce labor power. Just as coal shoveled into a boiler produces steam power.

Horse power is produced by transmitting hay and corn to the interior of a mule. Whatever it costs to produce the horse power of the mule will be the average wage of the mule.

The mule gets his pay in keep and the worker gets his keep in pay. This being the case the mules don't worry about the cost of living. But the worker, who gets his keep in pay, fools himself continually with the rummy idea that by cheap living he can make his wages go further or that higher wages will bring him on a level with the cost of living. All this don't bother the mule.

Let us say the mule gets twenty ears of corn per day. At one time his owner fed him more, but it only made him fat and lazy. At another time the boss fed him less and the mule got too weak to pull a load. So the boss settled down to feed the mule whatever corn was required to produce mule power. The amount was twenty ears per day.

If twenty ears of corn cost ten cents, then the wages of the mule expressed in money is ten cents per day.

One day a fine-looking fellow comes to the mule and says, "My name is Windyteddybillitaft. I am representing the grand old Republican party. I understand you are working for ten cents a day. Now this may be all right for the pauper mules of Europe, but no self-respecting American mule should work for such a wage. We have organized a political party for the benefit of mules. At present we are advocating a hundred per cent tariff on corn. As soon as this is accomplished the price of corn will double and you will get twenty cents per day instead of the measly ten cents you get now."

Wonder what the mule would say to that argument? Well, if he were just an ordinary four-footed mule he would say, "Windyteddybillitaft, I don't eat the noise, but the corn. I get the same quantity whether the price goes up or down because the boss found out I've got to have just so much or he'll have to pull the wagon himself." And then the mule would wink one eye and jokingly tickle the great statesman under the double chin with his left hind hoof.

Neither would he join the William Jennings Bryan marching club, even if the Democratic party has honored the mule by making him the patron saint of democracy. Cheap corn and free trade has as little attraction to a normal mule as high corn and tariff. But while we may be unable to rile up the mules on the tariff question the politicians had no such trouble with the workers. Four generations of toilers have chased the will-of-the-wisp tariff over the dismal swamp of American politics without ever being able to bring wages and the cost of living visibly nearer to each other.

Wage Slavery Versus Chattel Slavery

Chattel slavery never gained a good foothold in the north. Not that the pious New Englanders had any particular scruples about slavery. But the northern crops, wheat and corn, only required the services of workers during seeding and harvest time, at the outside not more than four months in the year. The interests of the grain farmers demanded laborers that could be bounced after the work was over. Industries too required workers who possessed at least a rudimentary education to enable them to read blueprints and follow written instructions. All these requirements were lacking in the African slave.

The staple product of the south is cotton. It takes thirteen months out of the year to raise a crop. It also takes the women out of the homes and the children out of school to do it. Hence, cotton and ignorance go together like ham and eggs. Slave labor is just what is needed to serve "king cotton." Yet chattel slavery is inferior to wage slavery. In the first place the slave-owner must buy the laborer before he can get his labor power. An able bodied field hand used to fetch anywhere from one to four thousand dollars. The northern employers could get all the laborers they needed for nothing.

Many of the slaves would run away from their masters. They had steady jobs, life-time jobs, but didn't have enough sense to appreciate "steady employment," and a small army of officials and bloodhounds were needed to catch the runaways.

Gentle reader, have you ever heard of a wage worker running away from a job? Is it not a fact that he is continually chasing a job? Even I, blessed with a superior intelligence as I am, have caught myself sleeping on the soft side of a freight car while chasing an elusive job over God's country. Don't you think that from this viewpoint of the employer at least, a system under which the worker chases the job, is preferable to a system where the boss must chase after the workers?

They used to drive the slaves out of bed in the morning with snake whips. Slaves have no particular incentive to cultivate early rising. It's of no use to sing to a slave, "Early to bed and early to rise makes a man healthy, wealthy and wise." He won't believe it. All he gets is a living. And like a sensible man he gets that with the least possible exertion.

Wage-workers, or free men, so-called because they don't cost anything, don't have to be chased out of bed in such a rude manner. They purchase alarm clocks and place them on dish-pans right next to the pillow on which loving hands have embroidered "Slumber sweetly."

They wind up their own infernal machines with which to hoist themselves out of bed. Now a system under which the workers drive themselves to work, beats a system all hollow under which the boss has to get up first and hustle out the workers.

When the boll worms took the cotton, the ignorant slaves used to sing "glory hallelujah, thar ain't gwine to be any work." Poor benighted heathens, they didn't appreciate the blessings of "plenty of work." Work or no work, their owners would give them food, clothing and shelter. We don't starve a valuable horse just because we haven't got anything for it to do. Do we?

But when the mine or shop closes down my previous free worker don't sing, "glory hallelujah, I'm out of a job." O no! He makes a face about two feet long and puts three whiskeys and four schooners under his freeman's belt before he musters up enough courage to break the news to mother. When the shop closes down, the boss turns his horses out on the grass and he turns his workers out on the street with instructions to "keep off the grass."

It used to be that when a slave got a pain in his inners, the slave-owner's boy would chase on the fastest horse to the best doctor in the country, while "ole missus" and her daughters would sit up night after night to nurse that three-thousand-dollar slave back to health.

The next time you suffer from an acute attack of indigestion caused from undereating and the wife of your boss and his two lovely daughters sit up with you while little Clarence Algernon tries to run down a ten thousand dollar specialist with a four thousand dollar touring car, let me know.

Yes, slavery had its drawbacks. Plenty of them. But the worst one was that the biggest part of the profit made out of the slaves was used up in buying new slaves.

The northern capitalist had no need to purchase new workers in place of those gone to the boneyards. And so the surplus value taken from the wage-workers accumulated as capital in the form of railroads, factories and machines. Chattel slavery didn't have a ghost of a show to keep up with wage slavery and the dear old south was left hopelessly behind in the race for supremacy.

Now it is a well proven historical fact, that the people who own the wealth of a nation soon will own its government, too. The southern slave-owners had run the government in their own interests. They had opposed railroad building, so essential to capitalist expansion, in the north. They had discouraged manufacture, fearing that a great factory population would furnish a market for the product of the northern farmers, thus raising the cost of feeding their own slaves. But over and above all, the south had bitterly opposed a protective tariff demanded by the northern capitalists. The tariff, more than any other factor, was responsible for the war between the north and the south. Of course Mary's little history says it was the desire of the good northern people to free the poor slaves from the oppression of the bad southern people that brought on this Civil War. But Mary's school history don't explain why abolitionists were persecuted in the north as much as in the south. It don't explain why Wendell Phillips and William Lloyd Garrison were mobbed in the streets of Boston. It don't explain why Lovejoy was lynched in a northern town.

If the Republican party or its cleanest, purest and most illustrious exponent, Abraham Lincoln, ever advocated abolition, then all proofs to this effect must have been destroyed. On the contrary, the war came in spite of the most earnest pledges of the government of Lincoln that *slavery would not be disturbed*.

If the Republican party was in favor of abolition, why then did the northern government furnish passes to southern-slave owners to pass through the federal lines clear up to 1863 to catch their runaway slaves?

How can "the war for the abolition of slavery" be explained in face of the fact that the Republican Congress passed a joint resolution in 1861, after eight southern states had seceded, declaring for a constitutional amendment, which forever would bar all further interference with slavery? No, no, the Republican party was not only willing that the southern slave-owners should retain their black property, but it was willing and anxious to make slavery a perpetual institution—provided only that the seceding states would return to the fold.

In looking for the cause of such gigantic upheavals as the war of secession, we must seek in other quarters than in the soft hearts of sentimentalists or the moral conscience of a few good men. That sentiment, morals and the sense of justice are factors which will influence human movements no one will deny. But these are not dominant or determining factors. The wind will affect the course of a bullet, but the general direction is determined by the marksman. So great human movements may be influenced by moral factors, but the determining force is material interest—the nickel under the foot.

The war of rebellion came, and had to come, because two economic systems, slavery and capitalism, could not exist under the same government. Each system demanded legislation for the protection of its interests. These interests were antagonistic. The struggle between the two systems became a struggle for the control of the government and inevitably had to lead to the destruction of the system that lost in the political struggle.

Why Workers War

No workingclass interests were at stake in the war between the north and the south. As already stated, it was a struggle between slave-owner and capitalist. At the bottom was the tariff question. But besides slave-owners and capitalists there were other people in this country.

In the south there was a large poor white population, contemptuously called "white trash" by the slave aristocracy. This class, comprising nearly nine-tenths of the total population of the south, tilled the hillside farms too poor to raise cotton. This class neither exported nor imported. In fact, it had precious little to buy, or to sell. Every hillside farm produced what it consumed and consumed what it produced. The poor white farmer raised a little corn, converted it into moonshine dew, or corn-pones and consumed it himself. He planted a little tobacco and cured, smoked, chewed or snuffed it. A few sheep furnished wool to be carded, spun and woven by the women folks, and the cloth was made into clothes by the same hands. A cow or two furnished milk while alive and meat and hide for shoes when dead.

These people made their own furniture, built their own shacks, and hammered together their own coffins. Outside of iron and salt, they were practically independent of the world's market. Few of them could vote. None could be elected to office. As a class they were despised not only by the slave-owners, but even by the slaves.

Yet, when the war broke out it was this poor, needy, illiterate, beggarly class that rushed to the defense of an economic system that had degraded them for generations.

What did these poor people have to do with free trade or tariff? If there was one class that could gain, materially, socially and politically through the annihilation of the slave power, it was the poor whites of the south. But instead of attending strictly to their own knittings, they fell all over themselves to furnish cannon fodder for people who held them in the utmost contempt. Owning nothing worth fighting for, they fought for principles, justice, God, fatherland, the flag of freedom, etc. Those who felt the necessity of more substantial reasons claimed that they were fighting for their slaves. Poor deluded dupes. They didn't have any slaves. Only about eight per cent of all the southern people possessed slaves. But men are not what they are, but what they think they are, and a man who has slaves on his brain will fight a darned sight harder than the gentleman who has slaves on his plantation. The Civil War furnishes ample proofs that Karl Marx was right, eternally right, when he said, "The ruling ideas of every period are the ideas of its ruling class."

Did the slave-owners go to war too? Sure thing. These gentlemen enjoying exemption from the sordid struggle for existence had but little work for their brain and consequently allowed this otherwise rather useful organ to sleep. They faced the approaching struggle with the same stupid bravado that a bull calf faces a locomotive. What idea did these gentlemen of leisure have about the strength of the north? To them the roaring furnaces, the fire-belching mills, the million-spindled looms, the miles of shining rails, the heaving iron horses, the modern catacombs of coal and metal, the harvesters and reapers had no significance. Living in another age, they dreamed of a struggle of muscle and brawn, when in reality it was a struggle between brute force, and brain and machine.

"The war will only last until after breakfast," or at any rate not more than thirty days, "stick a corn cob on a broom handle and poke it at a Yankee and he'll run," are samples of the assinine witticism indulged in by the empty-headed slaveocrats.

Under such pleasant circumstances it was only natural that the young society buds should don natty grey uniforms and as lieutenants, captains, colonels, majors and generals, lead the poor white trash into war. But unfortunately the war lasted over breakfast, dinner and supper. In fact, it soon dawned upon the aristocratic swells that war after all was hardly a place for refined folks. Worse and moreover, some of the nicest young men of the very best southern families actually got killed. And still worse got killed by people to whom they never had been even properly introduced. Something had to be done to save "the flower of the south." The government, always the hand-maid of the ruling classes, came to the rescue. After the fall of Fort Donnelson, the Confederate Congress composed of slave-owners and their lawyers, passed a series of acts which *exempted all men who owned more than twenty slaves from military service in the Confederate army.* The number of slaves required to exempt the owner later on was reduced to ten. Other property-owners who owned no slaves could escape service by paying certain stipulated sums or by rendering other than military service to the government. Needless to say the poor white trash was not consulted on a matter which made service in the Confederate army voluntary for the rich and compulsory for the poor.

It would not be fair to say that all slave-owners availed themselves of the exemption clause. Many fought to the end of the war like brave men. But many others did crawl home to mammy through the hole so conveniently provided by their government. It was not an uncommon practice then for big slave-owners to divide their slaves among their sons in order to keep them out of the war.

The southern trader class was looked down upon by the slave aristocracy. Moreover, this class had no direct interest in the struggle. At the same time, traders are entirely too sharp to risk their hides for such spooks as flags, principles, justice and eternal rights. To give this class something tangible to fight for, the Confederate Congress repudiated the debts owed by southern merchants to northern jobbers and manufacturers. Since this total indebtedness was estimated at between fifty and three hundred million dollars, we have sufficient reasons why the southern middle class fought for independence.

This class and the professionals, who stood to the slave-owners in about the same relation as the retainers of medieval times did towards the feudal lord, furnished most of the officers for the patriotic poor whites who were the only ones who had no nickels under their feet.

2260

A few miles west of Columbus, Ohio, is a pleasant wooded hill overlooking the Scioto Valley, Camp Chase.

During the Civil War it was a prison camp for Confederate soldiers. What kind of a prison camp it was is testified by the inscription on a huge boulder which serves as the only monument to the departed "boys in grey." It reads, "Here lie the remains of 2260 unknown Confederate soldiers." Two thousand two hundred and sixty human beings is a goodly number to be buried without somebody going to the trouble of ascertaining their names.

It must be remembered that these men did not expire on the bloody battlefield. They were not mowed down by the hail of bullets, Camp Chase was not a battle ground, but just one of those pleasant, cheerful, healthy prison camps nothern historians are so fond of telling about. Within two miles of the capital of the great state of Ohio, in view of many Christian church spires, these poor boys died of gangrene, lockjaw, and typhoid fever. Died by the dozens every night. And in all the land there was not one single man in authority interested enough to mark their resting place; to write a name on stone or board over their lonely graves. They were but workingmen. Common soldiers fighting the battles of a master class. Officers belonging to the "better class" rarely die in prison camps. They are exchanged, paroled, or at least harbored in more sanitary quarters.

I have been told by old Confederate soldiers who at one time were prisoners at Camp Chase, that they never saw one single commissioned Confederate officer call the roll in the morning to ascertain the names of the boys that had died during the night.

In peace or war we bear the burdens. Whatever fame and glory war may bring belongs to our masters. The workers share is festering wounds, lost limbs, ruined health, death and massed graves bearing the inscription "here lie. . .unknown men."

And yet some people knew and loved these "unknown men." Scattered over the sunny South from the valley of the Shenandoah, over the knobs of Tennessee, the clay banks of Mississippi, the swamps of Louisiana and the prairies of Texas, there were thousands of mothers and thousands of wives who waited anxiously from day to day, from month to month, from year to year for one who never came.

Seasons came and seasons went and still with hungry eyes they watched the lonely road for a figure that never turned into the bend. The north wind moaned mid fragrant pines, springtime came laughing in the land, the torrid heat of summer's sun burned on the cabin roof, the wild geese winged their way to the gulf, squirrels chattered in the burnished leaves and still they waited and waited in vain, and hoped and hoped against hope.

Wives laid awake in the dead of night in lonely hillside shacks. They listened not to the song of the mockingbird calling its mate in the moonlit night. They did not hear the southern breeze murmuring in the magnolia trees. They listed with aching, breaking hearts for footsteps they never heard again.

"War is hell." A rich man's war—a poor man's hell.

Life and Property

Have you ever heard of General Rockefeller or General Morgan, or Major Carnegie, Captain Vanderbilt or Colonel Gould? If not, why not? Was not service in the federal army compulsory? Did not all men over eighteen and under forty-five years of age have to pay the blood tax, that is, serve in the federal army?

Oh, no, gentle reader, dispel all delusions on that subject. *The law was so framed that all those who could afford the price of a substitute could stay at home.* The Republican party, then as now the tool of the capitalist class, took good care to protect the valuable lives of *property-owners.* It was only the landless, homeless, toolless proletarians that *had to serve.* It was optional with property-owners. They could serve if they wanted to. So most of them stayed at home like sensible long-headed businessmen and made hay while the sun shone, while permitting the miserable workers to pour out their lifeblood on southern battlefields.

Mark Hanna, at one time the high-priest of the Republican party, was engaged in the wholesale grocery business in Cleveland, Ohio, when the war broke out. As a leading businessman he had too many pressing engagements to find time for soldiering. He consequently hired a substitute, not for the grocery, but for the war business. And oh, grim humor, two years before Mark Hanna died, the Grand Army of the Republic elected him honorary member of that body. Maybe it was in honor of his substitute.

John D. Rockefeller had just then started on his oily career. As a rising young businessman he found better things to do than to kill, or what is worse, to be killed. He too fought in the most stupendous struggle of the 19th century through the medium of a substitute.

Pierpont Morgan was twenty-four years old when Lincoln called for volunteers. But although Mr.

Morgan's biographers inform us that he was a college athlete and of splendid physical make-up, he must have been hard of hearing, for Lincoln's call never reached him. Being of a rather practical turn of mind he entered business by buying condemned rifles from the government for $3.50 and selling them back to the same government for $22.50 a piece. It was a neat transaction for a young man. When the authorities finally woke up to the deal, they refused to pay the patriotic gentleman, whereupon he promptly brought legal action against the government. The Supreme Court of the U.S. finally handed down a decision which gave Morgan the full amount claimed. Had Morgan been a poor man he most likely would have swung for high treason.

Andrew Carnegie got as far as the battle of Bull Run. I don't know whether this celebrated conflict was named after the marvelous run made by Andy or not. But Andy ran, and he never quit running until he got back to Pennsylvania where he bought a substitute to fill his unexpired term as a hero in the Federal Army.

This list could be kept up almost indefinitely and it would include practically every principal businessman who was old enough to serve in the army in 1861 to 1865.

No, I do not say that every rich man or every rich man's son escaped service in the same way. But I do say that as a class, the property-owners of the north utilized the government instituted for the protection of property, to exempt property-owners from military duty in the Civil War.

The law which exempted property-owners was as rank a piece of class legislation as ever was enacted, but it did not say in so many words, "poor people must go to war, rich folks may."

No, no! we are all equal before the law. We have no classes in this country and so the law expressly said, "All must serve over and below a certain age"—except those who can afford to buy substitutes. In a free country like ours, farm hands, ditchdiggers and factory workers have as much right as the Rockefellers, Carnegies, Goulds and Morgans to buy substitutes. It is true, they may lack the money to do so, but that is their own *fault*.

It was not necessary to draft all the workers into the Federal Army. Lots of them went of their own accord. Whole labor union locals, for instance, joined in a body. If anyone wants to know why these poor devils went to war be it known that they fought for their country. It is true that they had no country. Some of them paid a few pennies per week to burial associations and industrial insurance companies to buy a country in the form of a cemetery lot. But these were of the more ambitious kind. The others only had boarding houses to fight for. All of them fought for the flag. When a fellow has nothing else to fight for he usually fights for "the flag." He always can say "my flag" even if it don't belong to him. That's what flags are for.

Besides this, the propertyless worker's children went to war. Over one-half of all the soldiers of the Union Army were boys under twenty years of age. Poor foolish boys, who were lured from home and mother by the sight of tinseled brass-buttoned uniforms and the sound of drum, fife and bugle. They led the poor children to death and destruction, even as the ratcatcher of Hamlin led the children of that ancient burg out of the city gate never to return again.

Would it not be more honorable to place the statue of a round-eyed, round-cheeked boy on top of the soldiers' monument, in place of that bearded man who stands there now? Would it not be more honorable and truthful—or, are we ashamed of the boy scouts of 1861, "the soldier *boys*" and the *boys* in blue as we called them then?

Thus it happened that the man without a slave, killed the man without a country, and the man without a country killed the man without a slave, while the slave-owners and capitalists, as a class, remained at home.

War and the Church

We are a Christian nation. Christianity is the religion of peace. Its founder came to bring "peace on earth, good will to men." While living he preached peace and love. "Love thy neighbors, love thy enemies"; "those who live by the sword shall perish by the sword," are a few of the sayings of the carpenter of Nazareth. Let us see how his self-styled followers conducted themselves during the bloody brothers' war between north and south, between capitalism and slavery.

For four years the ignorant workers killed each other by the hundred thousands. The blood of the murdered toilers soaked the ground on a hundred battlefields. The voices of dying legions rose to heaven. Did then the organized church rise in one mighty protest against the carnage, against this slaughtering of the innocent? No!

The church, like every other human institution, is but a creature of its environment. Those who can rise above their environment are exceptions. And the organized church is not an exception; it never rises above its worldly environment.

Today we say slavery is wrong. But there was a time when slavery was legally, morally and ethically right. To free a slave was theft. To incite slaves to free themselves was a violation of the law. The slave-owner sat in the front pews of the churches and paid the salaries of the clergy. Hence the latter interpreted the sacred writings in the interests of the slave-owners, and preached sermons in defense of slavery. The laws of God, as well as the laws of man, were used to support the slave system.

Even before the outbreak of actual hostilities, the dominant religious denominations—Methodists, Baptists and Presbyterians—split into two camps. The Mason and

Dixon line was not only the dividing line between Capitalism and Slavery, it also divided religious organizations into warring factions. And each faction attached itself to the ruling class of its section and became its mouthpiece, defender and apologist. Thus we find men who derive their inspiration from the same bible preaching slavery in the south and abolition in the north.

To murder is wrong, everybody will admit that. The good book says, "Thou shalt not kill." That's plain, isn't it? Now I don't want to be finicky about killing. I don't want to go too far. For instance, it may be all right for a white man to kill a Negro because the Creator has painted one white and the other black. Dislike of the other fellow's color may be a perfectly legitimate excuse for killing him. At least this seems to be the accepted idea of some people.

It also may be allowable for one white man to kill another white man providing the latter is a heathen. Heathens, as everybody knows, go to hell anyhow and whether they go there a little sooner or later should not make much difference.

It may even be all right for a white Christian German to kill a white Christian Frenchman. It is true that both are Caucasians and pray to the same God. But they make a different noise about it and there is just a possibility that God does not like the other fellow's gibberish. But when white Christians, speaking the same language and worshiping in the same temples, kill each other by the wholesale for four years then I say "this is going too far." And when I read, that with every regiment of soldiers there traveled a minister of the gospel who prayed to the *allvater* in heaven to bless our arms, that is, to give us strength to press the bayonet into the quivering flesh of our brother, to steady our arms and clear our eyes, so that we may send the little leaden messenger of death into the breast of another one of God's children—then, again, I say this is going too far.

Yes, even the church must obey the economic law which says, *whatever is to the interest of the strongest class in society, is right.* When workingmen once understand that the actions of the organized church are not determined by its religious teachings, professions and traditions, but by the economic material interests of its clergy, then they will learn that religion and church are two distinct things. They will also then be careful not to take their politics from the same source that they take their religion.

Full Dinner Pail

Money and Doughnut Issues

One of the first laws enacted by the Republican Congress was a high protective tariff measure, the so-called war tariff. The Confederate government had practically adopted the whole of our federal constitution with the addition of a plank which prevented the Confederation from levying a tariff for the protection of industries. Here are two characteristic acts which more than anything else show the real difference between capitalists and slave-owners.

The old game of paying the working people and soldiers with depreciated paper money was also resurrected. The government issued a currency that was good for any debt, private or public. But it was not good to pay revenues with. In other words the government said, "Here is my note, but don't bring it back to me. My note is payable by anybody but myself."

That such money should depreciate to forty cents on the dollar was a foregone conclusion. When the boy in blue received his thirteen dollars at the end of the month they represented about five dollars in gold. But when the speculators and bankers presented the same pieces of paper to Uncle Sam a few years afterwards, he gladly paid good hundred-cent dollars for the pretty pieces of paper which our monied people had acquired for forty cents apiece.

If I had the space I would go into the money question more thoroughly, not because this question is of any great importance to our kind, but just to show what infernal monkeys the workers can make of themselves over things that do not concern them.

You all remember the time back in '96 when we used to stand around the streetcorner and argue money. We talked mighty big about inflated currency, the intrinsic value of money and the unlimited coinage of silver at the ratio of 16 to 1. To hear us then, one would have concluded that handling money was our specialty, when in fact we poor devils talked of gold and silver and did not even have coppers in our pockets. Fellows who could not have found Europe on the map, or were not able to tell the difference between Europe and a turnip, wanted dollars that were good in Europe. We talked of sound money to beat the band, and all we got was the sound. William Jennings Bryan is about the only man who ever got anything out of the money question.

When they didn't talk money to us they rung in tariff for a change. They painted a full dinner pail, with a chicken leg sticking out from under the lid, on a canvas, and then we made a grab for a greasy torch and ran after the prosperity parade, with coal oil soaking into our scalps. We know now what the tariff has done to us, how it has protected us from the pauper laborers of Europe. All we have to do is to look over the wire entanglement around the high protected steel mill and watch Stanislaus Slawinsky and Rinando Rinaldini fooling away twelve hours per day, seven days in the week, at two per day, where we used to get a five spot for a day's work.

Our good friends, the bosses, kept the pauper labor product out of the country all right enough, only they brought the pauper laborer over to take our jobs and our be-lov-ed American standard of living. But don't kick, brother worker, you are not a bit more foolish than the farmers who voted for a high protective tariff on everthing they bought and for free trade on every thing they sold. Get rid of that faraway gaze; that fried chicken leg sticking out of the full dinner pail was only a symbol; something to hold up to simples you know. Of course I don't think we could lead a donkey all over creation with the picture of a bale of hay; but thank God we are not mules, but free born independent American workingmen.

The last political campaign was fought out on a doughnut. It was a painted doughnut to be sure, but it looked natural as life and below it said, "look at the doughnut, don't look at the hole." Mr. Taft, on the recommendation of Mr. Roosevelt, rolled into office on the doughnut rim and left us the hole to digest.

I don't know what the next great (?) issue will be. Most likely the tariff. But one thing is sure—it will not be an issue concerning the working class. And yet, the workers have their own demands and their own particular interests.

Proletarian Issues

Even before the Civil War there was a labor movement in this country. The workers who no longer owned their tools, but became more and more hands tending machines that belonged to the capitalist class, organized unions to obtain a larger share of the product of their labor.

In the early days of unionism they fought for the establishment of free schools and the abolition of imprisonment for debts, as well as higher wages and shorter hours. The demands of the unionists, briefly stated, have been Higher Wages, Shorter Hours and Abolition of Child Labor. The means for attaining these ends was the strike.

Is it not singular that none of these proletarian demands found their way into the platforms of the two dominant political parties? Here was something the workers wanted so badly that they spent millions of dollars and suffered hunger, cold, imprisonment and even death to obtain. Thousands of strikes have been fought for the eight-hour day alone. But if one searches the platforms of the two old parties for a plank saying, "We demand the legal eight-hour day in the industries of the United States," he looks in vain.

Congress could establish a minimum wage; it could pass a national Child Labor Law. But neither of these two demands of labor were ever incorporated into national platforms. Then, when the workers took matters into their own hands and struck for better conditions, all the powers of municipal, state and national government were used to suppress the uprising. The political parties that had loudly advocated high tariff, free trade, gold standard, free silver, protection for the American standard of living, and what-not, in the interest of the workers, became the pliant tools of their capitalist masters and willingly supplied police, militia, regular army and court injunctions for the suppression of the strike. As a strike-breaker and general utility-man for the prevention of higher wages and lower hours, your Uncle Sam easily ranks first. What little improvement the workers have obtained for their class was obtained not with the help but in spite of the most brutal opposition of their own government.

If today we may still boast of a higher standard of living, if the American workingman is still able to fight for a grander civilization, don't thank those who directed the ship of state, but come with me to the lonely graves of the pioneers of unionism. No marble shaft rears proudly above the humble resting place. No monument in stone or bronze tells of their mighty deeds. But under the green sod sleep hearts that once flamed for the cause of toil. Martyrs of Labor, you have given more to liberty, equality and human brotherhood, than all the statesmen of this land combined. You have fought battles for a greater cause than all the soldiers that ever bled on battlefields. You have brought our race nearer to the great ideal of brotherhood of which Buddha dreamed on the Ganges three thousand years ago. In you, the thoughts of Plato and the teachings of the lowly Nazarene assumed reality. Like Moses of yore, you lead the children of toil from bondage out into the desert of strife, nearer and nearer to the promised land. And like the great Hebrew Prophet you laid your weary bodies down to eternal rest in sight of Canaan. Your reward was hunger and cold and the prison stripes and gallows. Some day a grateful posterity will chant chorals in your memory. Some day happy children will plant roses on your sunken graves. Humble tools of evolution, you have done more for civilization and the humanization of our race than all the statesmen, warriors and priests. To you our praise.

Conclusion

What is wrong with the man who fights against a tax on tea and who never experienced the pleasure of tasting it? What's wrong with the man who goes to war for slaves he does not own? What's wrong with him who goes forth to kill his brother in defense of a country that belongs to others? What's wrong with the fellow who wants a dollar "that's good in Europe" when he lives in Stringtown on the Pike? Its brain trouble, brother. From our eyebrows down we're workingmen and the capitalists have even gone so far as to uniform us in a distinct class garb (blue overalls) so that anyone may readily tell where we belong. But above our eyebrows in the hollow space between the hair, we are landlords, taxpayers, slave-owners and capitalists. The human brain is like a phonograph record. Whatever you talk in talks out, and the wrong people talked into our brain tanks. Those who write books and papers; those who print pictures and deliver orations and sermons, as a rule, receive their pay from those who own and control the wealth of a nation. Consequently they must espouse the interests of their employers or starve. Thus it came about, that the workers absorbed ideas into their brains, which were contrary to the interests of the rest of their bodies. They did not realize that they formed a class of their own with separate and distinct class interests. There was never a war or a political campaign fought in the history of this country in which proletarian interests were the issue. Yet we furnished both the bulk of the soldiers and the majority of the votes. We were but cat's paws in the hands of ruling classes. Of all the people, we were the only ones who were not *class conscious.* Yet no one will doubt that we have class interests, and that our class interests are opposed to the interests of other classes, mainly the capitalist class. We want higher, and the boss wants lower wages. We want a lower cost of living and the capitalists want higher prices. We want our children in school and the boss wants them in the factory. We organize unions of our own class and strike against our employers, while he hires thugs, scabs, detectives and strikebreakers to beat us.

In our Union halls we find a little round hole in the door through which we whisper the pass word. We have hand grips and rituals. We do all that man can do to keep the capitalists, their spies, and lawyers out of our union meetings. We are *class conscious* enough on the industrial field, but when it comes to sending men to the legislature or the Congress to make laws for us, we not only vote with the same people we fight during our strikes, but we even elect men whom we would under no consideration permit to enter our union meetings.

Chickens would not vote for coyotes, pigs would not vote for butchers, but we, the workers, have no objections to casting our ballots for men whose campaign expenses are paid by Morgan, Ryan, Carnegie and others who have crushed, with iron heels, every attempt of labor to improve its condition.

The strategic position in every class war is the government. No great improvement in the life of the toilers can be accomplished as long as this institution is in the hands of our enemies. The industrial struggle must be carried onto the political field. We must use our political power as well as the strike and the boycott.

But striving for political power must not prevent us from developing our other fighting organs to a higher degree of efficiency. We must strive ceaselessly to break down the barriers which divide the workers into petty cliques, each one following its own narrow aims to the detriment of the whole body of labor. The phrase, "an injury to one is the concern of all," must be more than a catchword. Above all else we must educate—educate our kind. "Knowledge is Power." Science, which has been such a powerful factor in the development of industrial life, must lend its torch to light the path of labor in the struggle for emanicipation.

Education, Agitation, Organization. Let these be the stars of hope, the cloud of smoke, the pillar of fire, to lead us into the promised land.

Every child returned to school, every hour of toil cut from the weary day, every dollar in wages gained, every scientific book read, every educational lecture heard, are so many building stones in the structure of the future.

The freedom of workers will come as a necessary result of the freeing of their minds from capitalistic influences. *Conscious* of our class interest we will soon recognize that there can be no equality without equality of opportunity; that there can be no freedom without the right to work; that there can be no justice unless each worker receives the full and undivided product of his toil; and having recognized this, we will learn, that the final emancipation of the producing class, can only be accomplished when the principal means of production, have passed from the hands of the few into the possession of the state; a state which is no longer a class tool for the protection of private property, but the trustee, guardian, and administrator of the *Commonwealth*.

The means to the end is the class struggle, but the goal itself is the abolition of classes and class wars though the establishment of the common ownership of the means of production. The place of the present industrial monarchy will be taken by the industrial democracy of the future, the Socialist Republic.

★ ★ ★